WHEN I
DON'T LIKE
MYSELF

YOUTH FORUM SERIES

A YOUTH FORUM BOOK

WHEN I DON'T LIKE MYSELF

by
William E. Hulme

THOMAS NELSON INC.
New York / Camden

Foreword

This book is one of a series in a unique publishing effort in which Youth Research Center, Inc., Minneapolis, Minnesota, has joined with Thomas Nelson Inc., Camden, New Jersey. The books are based on the very real concerns, problems, aspirations, searchings and goals of young people today as measured by nation-wide surveys being conducted continuously by the research center.

Central to the series is the belief that we all have a compelling need to turn to a core of faith for guidelines in coping with the world in which we live. Each book deals with a specific need or concern of young people viewed in relation to the Christian faith. By drawing upon the results of the surveys, each author is helped to speak more directly to the conflicts, values and beliefs of today's young people.

The significance of this series is enhanced, as well, by the scholarship and commitment of the authors. The grasp of the field in which each writes lends authority to his work and has established this series as a basic reference eagerly read and appreciated by young people.

Contents

WHEN I
DON'T LIKE
MYSELF

1. Society In Conflict

In the spring of 1970, 11 of the 14 regents
professors of the University of Minnesota—my
own state—went to Washington, D. C., at
their own expense to talk with government officials. A
regents professorship is the highest honor bestowed by the
University upon distinguished professors. Speaking as a
group for the first time in their history, these professors
were concerned that government officials did not realize
the extent of the alienation from the entire American
political system of the "sober, absolutely nonviolent majority of students."

1. *Conflict Between What Is and What Should Be in*
Society

Obviously there is a conflict between the way things are
and what we believe they should be in our society. In what
is probably the largest generation gap in many years, the
young people have made our entire society aware of its
failures. Our unsolved problems are literally tearing us
apart. We have never been so seriously divided since the
Civil War.

First of all is the problem of war. We have gone from a
day when the United States' role in war was justified, if

not glorified, to a day when it is exposed as deviously motivated and denounced as immoral, if not hypocritical. When two-thirds of our taxes are used to support war, as in Vietnam, the criticism is hitting us in the soft underbelly of our priorities.

Then there is the race problem. For generations the majority of white Christians have accepted the second class citizenship of the black, brown, and red people in our midst. Now the evil in the system has been exposed, but rectifying it is proving to be a monstrously complicated problem. In the meantime, the hatred between the races is —if anything—increasing.

Closely associated with the racial problem is the problem of the poor. Most of the millions of poor people are not in our churches. Instead, their antagonism toward the affluent who do attend our churches accounts for another of our agonizing divisions. In spite of well-meaning anti-poverty programs, the problem seems no closer to solution. Perhaps as some have suggested it is a problem of the affluent rather than of the poor.

If affluence is a problem, society's materialistic values would be one of its symptoms. The current attack upon this materialism is coming less from our pulpits than from our young people. As a group, they are not as enmeshed in the compromises and obligations that have ensnared their parents. Perhaps, also, young people today feel more free to evaluate and to challenge the values of the adult world. At any rate, the love of money—for the things it buys and the power it brings—is still a root, if not the root, of evil and certainly a motivation, if not the motivation, for most of our distorted sense of priorities.

There is also the pollution of our environment. This has

been going on for a long time but now—again thanks largely to young people and a few ecological prophets—we are becoming aware of its threat to our very existence. Yet our polluting ways are quite set—and buttressed by our materialistic values—so that effecting a change in time to salvage our planet is becoming an anxious challenge.

We are divided today not only by these problems but also by our ideas concerning how to solve them. Some say that the contrast between what is and what should be is so great that we have to destroy the entire structure—often called "the system"—so that a new structure can be erected upon the ruins. Others—quite obviously the majority—maintain that this approach is basically destructive and can end only in anarchy and chaos. Instead, they say, we should work within the system. Our democratic process contains the potential for change. Therefore it is the mark of wisdom to use it to effect change. So it is either a redistribution of our resources and powers—or a fruit basket upset!

But there are other voices among our youth. They also are concerned with the contrast between the way things are and the way they should be. But they are primarily concerned about this contrast as it exists in their personal lives. At a church youth group planning session, for example, a girl spoke against what she felt was an overemphasis on world and social problems to the exclusion of concern for the personal shortcomings she felt in herself and suspected in the rest of the group. Her point could be a reaction to an "overemphasis," as she herself indicated. It also could be the expression of an acute need —the need to come to terms with the misgivings she felt over her own self.

2. The Contrast Between the "Is" and the "Should" in Each of Us

Perhaps you—my reader—have some of these same misgivings. You, too, may know what it is like to be pained by the conflict between the *is* and the *should* in your own life. Maybe it is a sharp pain, since you know all too well what it is you would like to change—what you are doing that you wish you would not do, or what you are not doing that you wish you would. Perhaps, however, your awareness is less precise. Instead you may have a vague but uncomfortable sense of dissatisfaction—basically with yourself. Perhaps you wish there *were* something more definite.

This awareness of dissatisfaction—whether pin-pointed or diffuse—is what is meant by guilt. The current impression is that guilt is a handicap—something that interferes with our freedom. Despite our distaste for it, guilt does not go away. Instead, it takes on different forms and continues to inflict us.

If you are like most people, there are times when your negative feelings about yourself seem to overwhelm you. You become depressed by what you see when you look at yourself. When you see yourself primarily as incompetent, or dull, or insincere, or mean, or selfish, or perverted, or worthless or phoney, you know the conflict between what is and what should be.

At such a moment you may see no positive value in the way you feel. Yet feeling depressed and defeated is not the purpose of guilt. From any logical point of view, an awareness of contrast between what is and what should be would be the first—and necessary—step for growth. How can there be improvement unless one becomes aware of where improvement is needed? Guilt is precisely this awareness. As such it can be an impetus for change—and change for the better.

3. *The Conflict in Society and in the Self*

Since the conflict in society is so similar to the conflict within the individual, there must be a connection between the two. Is one but the reflection of the other? If so, where is the place to begin—with society or with our self? Or does each have its own indigenous setting so that they are completely different?

Actually, we can get lost in either direction. It is possible to project our personal problems on to society's ills and wage a displaced battle. While we may do some good in this manner, our own problems will keep getting in the way of any constructive effort to help society. By the same token we can turn inward upon our own ills and become indifferent or even oblivious to our responsibilities to society. Our preoccupation with our own pains is actually an impediment to any constructive effort to help ourselves.

Obviously the two areas must be kept separate in terms of our specific concentration for improvement. At the same time there is a connection between the two—society and the individual. In fact, we can refer to the one as the macrocosm—the large (macro) world (cosmos)—and to the other as the microcosm—the small (micro) world. In recognizing this connection between the two worlds and relating ourselves to it, we will be doing what is best for improvement in both areas.

4. *Concentration upon the Microcosm*

Though I am aware of the connection between the world of society and the world of the person, the emphasis of this book is upon the microcosm. We shall concentrate on the contrast between the *is* and the *should* in the life of the individual—in your life—that causes us to dislike ourselves. We shall not do this as an escape from our challenges, but as a means for meeting them more constructively.

Our purpose is to become free from the *need* for an escape. Our first concern is to come to grips with a decision regarding our own worth. As unique individuals, as persons, each of us is confronted continually by this decision. Much of what happens in terms of our involvement and achievement stems from the way in which we respond to this decision. Consequently we hope to avoid the temptation to use society's ills as a way of establishing meaning for our lives. Instead, our goal is to contribute to these problems our own individual sense of identity—of meaning.

Still, there is a mutuality here. Meaning does not hang in mid-air. It is applied to the challenges that confront us. We have a need not only to receive but to give—to contribute. When this need is satisfied, our sense of worth and of meaning is further enhanced.

But right now—when you don't like yourself—you are having a problem over your identity—who you are. This in turn creates a problem over meaning. What purpose is there for living? Even the "successful" may not know. One of our recent crop of young actors to hit the top in Hollywood said at the peak of his success, "I don't know of any reason to live."

The question of purpose pertains to our sense of worth. Do I, in my uniqueness, have anything—really—to contribute? The question also concerns meaning in general. Is there anything of value—of worth—to which I can really give myself?

Why should people have trouble liking themselves? Why is this such a problem in our day? What is there about a human being that makes this a distinctly human problem? It would seem only natural to assume that any form of life with the power to accept would begin first by accepting its own being. Not so with men. One might also assume that a person would enjoy his own company. Yet the opposite is more often the case. Consequently we search for distractions from boredom, escapes from pain, and relief from conflict through distractions and stimulants.

Our basic need is to deal directly with our conflict over our own self—the contrast between the way we are and the way we would like—or feel obligated—to be.

2. The Low Self-Image

We are more likely to be aware of the conflict between the *is* and the *should* as a dull nagging ache rather than a sharp pain. If we think about this ache, we may see that down deep underneath, in the inward recesses of our soul, we don't think very highly of our self. It is an unpleasant realization and most of us do not care to dwell upon it. Instead, we are easily distracted into directing our energies toward other activities.

These activities are symptoms of the conflict we are reluctant to face. Such symptoms are not the same for everyone. In fact, they can be the direct opposite in characteristics. One young man, for example, is a fierce competitor. In a group he tends to blurt out his opinions so emphatically that those who think differently feel overpowered by the sheer force of his presence. Sensing this, he often feels guilty afterwards and vows to restrain himself lest he ride rough-shod over those less capable of asserting themselves. The forces within him, however, are stronger than his mental resolves. In moments of disagreement, making his point becomes more important than being patient with others. In the counseling situation with the pressure of competition removed, he saw what was pushing him.

"I'm fighting against a fear," he said, "the fear that I'm *nothing.*"

On the other hand, a young woman with a similar

problem is no competitor at all. At school she procrastinates in the writing of assignments, often until it is too late. Rather than submit anything she does to the judgment of others, she withdraws.

"I guess I think I'm pretty worthless," she said in a moment of truth. "If I do something—or say something and am criticized for it, I get terribly depressed." As a defense, she became a rebel against all "requirements." "If I can do what I want to do rather than what somebody else wants me to do, I can be my own judge of what I do."

Despite the difference in the symptoms, the problem is the same. We call it by a new name today—the *low self-image*. Formerly it was the inferiority complex. Both terms mean a negative self-evaluation. *Inferior* implies a comparison with *superior*, and *low*, a contrast to *high*. Though the individual makes the judgment, it is a socially-conditioned judgment.

Youth Research Center in Minneapolis, Minnesota, for a decade has investigated the needs of youth. It has accumulated data concerning young people from hundreds of church congregations of various denominations. The conclusions indicate that the low self-image is the underlying problem in youth. I think it would be safe to say that it is also basic to adult frustration. In fact, the low self-image is the current cultural expression of guilt. Perhaps this is why we are having such difficulty in coping constructively with it: we do not recognize it as guilt and consequently do not apply our traditional resources for dealing with guilt. Or are these resources no longer applicable? Are we so achievement-prone, do our aspirations so far exceed our attainments that they are more frustrating than inspiring? In any case, the low self-image in itself provides no motivation to achieve.

Yet persons with low self-images *can* achieve. Some of

us are blessed with special talents in areas which, since our earliest memories, have escaped the debilitating effects of defeat. These abilities can become substitutes for self-worth. For some it is *grades*. These young people have the ability to do well in school and depend upon their scholastic achievements for their sense of self-worth. Others depend upon their athletic ability. They live for sports because they enjoy them, but also because they find in them their identity.

Still others have a way with people, a personal charm which is captivating. As with those with the ability to do well in school or in sports, they may depend upon their *personality*. They use it to get by.

Those who lack other talents may try to excel in sex. Their sense of worth stems from the appreciation they receive from others for their sexual abilities. As one girl put it, "In adolescence I discovered that I had sex appeal. It was at least—and at last—something I could be good at."

In each of these ways—and more—skills are used to substitute for the person. What should then enhance the self-image may only mark the contrast. This is because the skills have developed apart from self-worth, rather than as an expression of it. By becoming the means by which we receive the needed appreciation from others, the skill leaves the naked self all the more isolated. The transfer from the skill to the self fails to take place because the skill is actually a compensation for the self—the person. Without the skill, the person would feel he were nothing.

The theological counterpart of this contrast between the skill and the person is that between grace and works. St. Paul said, "By grace you have been saved . . . not because of works." (Eph. 2:8–9). St. James said, "Faith by itself, if it has no works is dead." (James 2:17). Churches have at times become divided over emphasizing grace or works.

Actually both Paul and James are right. Grace and works are both necessary, but they are not simply parallel ways. Grace means God's love, his favor, which is given directly to us. Works are like skills which reveal our talents and often bring appreciation from others. We are justified in God's sight by his grace, without conditions such as accomplishments or works. Works refer to our achievements. Fortunately we are not justified by these—that is, they do not establish our worth. Rather, they give expression to it —and enhance it.

Such works grow out of the experience of being justified —valued, loved—as a person, a unique person, without having to prove our worth. Otherwise we may feel we are loved only for our works, skills, accomplishments, and hence not really loved at all. Yet works are necessary since we must be contributors as well as receivers. The progression is not complete until the grace that makes us secure also makes us productive.

2. Awareness of the Conflict—Sharp

Not all guilt goes unrecognized. Your low self-image may be based upon something very specific. Perhaps you have a "besetting sin" which you have been trying in vain to overcome. Or you may be a poor competitor in spirit and "chicken out" rather than put your abilities to the test. Afterward you dislike yourself for being such a fearful saboteur of your own progress. You *know* why your self-esteem is low.

Others may be convinced that they are unattractive as persons. They confuse their person with their personality, and see themselves as *blah*. When they try to be more personable, they feel self-conscious, and their efforts seem awkward. They may not call it guilt, but they know why they don't like themselves.

Closely associated with the pain of self-consciousness is the feeling that one is weak. In contrast, others seem strong and therefore in the dominant position, able to accept or reject someone else. This makes a person feel dependent rather than interdependent; he loses his identity in being overly concerned about the impression he is making. "I can't say no, even when I want to," is the way one young man put it. "I'm so terribly hung up on wanting to be liked that I can't be myself—whoever that is!" He knows why he doesn't like himself. He also knows why he feels guilty after lacking the courage to assert himself. His failure is the focus of his conflict between the *is* and the *should*.

3. *Impotence before the Conflict*

One would assume that being aware of the contrast between the way things are with us and the way they should be, even though depressing, would move us to take the necessary steps to close the gap. If we know specifically what it is that we wish to change, the assumption is that we would go to work in this direction. If our awareness is vague so that we feel the discomfort without specifically knowing why, it would be logical for us to attempt to locate the causes for our discomfort.

If something is wrong with your car, you are concerned about getting it fixed. If you are good with motors, you give things the "once-over" to locate the trouble. If you get stuck, you ask your dad, or somebody else who knows as much or more about cars than you do. You stick to it until the trouble is remedied, until the contrast between the *is* and the *should* is overcome.

So also if something is wrong with the bread or the cake you are baking. If it doesn't rise, you try and figure out why. If you are stumped, you ask your mother or somebody else who knows about baking. You get a few ideas and try again, until the product is what it should be.

But this is not what normally happens when the problem is our *self*. Here the gap between the *is* and the *should* tends to become fixed: the depression it creates within us saps our energies and leaves us in the dregs of defeat. We become immobilized by the feeling that we are going in circles and get bogged down in the rut of senseless repetition. We can't seem to take hold—or even to ask for help. As a result, we "spin our wheels."

Ours is a day that emphasizes progress. This is why more young people are attracted to college. Some feel it's the thing to do to get ahead, to get the right jobs, to be somebody important, and they feel they need that diploma. Thus many are uptight about what to do with their lives. The opportunities have increased and with them the responsibility to decide. It must have been easier when a boy was expected to follow his father's trade and a girl to fulfill herself in marriage and motherhood. Yet I doubt if you would want to go back to those days, even though the opportunities to make your own decisions can be frightening—particularly when the pressure is *on*.

We hear adults speak about this or that youth as *promising*. They mean that he seems to have what it takes to "get somewhere" or "go places." They express that subtle pressure placed upon young people that I imagine you, too, have felt. Maybe you have a brother or sister who is doing well at school, either with grades or with athletics or in student body leadership or in popularity. Perhaps, also, you sense your parents' pride in this brother or sister and wonder whether they are disappointed in you by comparison. These pressures aggravate even further the frustration we experience over our self and our lack of progress. As a result, the gap may become even more fixed between the *is* and the *should*.

4. *Lost in the Woods*

The frustration is best expressed by the familiar analogy of being lost in the woods. In tramping through the woods, the hiker realizes he is lost. Striving to get his bearings, he heads in what he believes is the right direction. As he continues along what seems to be a straight course, his hopes rise, for he should soon be coming into the clear. But the clearing does not appear. Instead he slowly becomes aware of tell-tale signs—things he has seen before. Is he? No, it can't be! Yet the evidence increases. He is back where he was when he first realized he was lost. He has been going in a circle!

There are those moments of awful truth when we recognize the tell-tale signs and realize that despite all our energies, we have gone nowhere. The illusions of progress are exposed. We have been going in a circle. In the anguish of despair, what happens to our hope?

Perhaps you know about this from personal experience. Perhaps it has happened to you repeatedly. Slowly or suddenly you have realized you were going nowhere. All hopes for progress collapsed in one big defeat. You felt the mockery of life as you saw that what had looked like a straight line was actually a circle. In your social life—in your school work—in your family relationships—in your personality problems—in your personal weaknesses—in your besetting sins—in your bad habits—in your prayer life—getting nowhere! Here is the feeder for the low self-image. How can one like a failure—even when it is himself? The low self-image is the image of the disliked self.

The irony of such experiences is not only that what seemed like progress turned out to be an illusion, but that we allow ourselves to get caught in this trap again and again. We would think that once would be enough and after this we would make sure that it didn't happen again. A hiker in the woods probably would do so. But not so the liver of life. In this role, we tend to repeat our failures.

3. The Repetition Compulsion

Sigmund Freud observed in his patients a tendency to repeat their failures and called it the "repetition compulsion." Referring to it as a "compulsion with a hint of possession of some 'daemonic' power," he noted it was likely to be experienced with behavior over which one has misgivings.* Ironically, we repeat what we really do not like. We seem destined to redo rather than to overcome. Although guilt is the evidence of misgivings, it is more often the stimulus to repeat rather than to change—to perpetuate the gap between the *is* and the *should*, rather than to close it.

Another analyst, Karen Horney, interpreted this same tendency as the "security of the familiar." When we repeat something, we become familiar with it. This very familiarity moves us to repeat it again. The word "familiar" comes from the word "family." It means to "be at home with." There is security in the family. There is also a time to leave the family. As we grow into adulthood, we make the change—often frightening—of leaving home. When we marry, we start a new home. But to do this, we need to leave—psychologically as well as physically—the old home. "Therefore a man leaves his father and his mother and cleaves to his wife." (Gen. 2:24). Yet the security of

* Sigmund Freud, *Beyond the Pleasure Principle*, New York: Bantam Books, 1959, page 67.

the old—the familiar—prevents some people from leaving. Attached to the old, they are not free to establish the new. The familiar is the *is*. We have been that way before, and so it is easy to replay it. Take the family quarrel, for example. Do you tangle with your brother or sister? If so, I imagine each time sounds like a rerun. The same might be said for your arguments with your mother or father or theirs with each other. I pick this example because family quarreling stimulates quite a bit of guilt. We would like to get along better with those whom we supposedly love.

Yet the familiarity of the pattern is so entrenched through repetition that each participant's role in the quarrel is well worked out. You fall into your role without even thinking about it. You say the same things in the same way, almost as if it had been rehearsed. It has— many times! This is why at least two "players" are needed. As much as you may not like your role, you are familiar with it. It provides you with a certain security. And we all like—and need—security.

In contrast, the *should* is often virgin territory. It contains the unknown in contrast to the known. Though we desire it, we also may shy away from it. Human beings have an inherent fear of the unknown. The terms we use for the unknown are significant. We fear the *stranger*. The word "strange" means "unfamiliar." It also means "alien," which in turn means the opposite of intimacy—of family. When close associates have a falling-out, we say they have become estranged. These words mean that which is different, other, foreign; they have a negative connotation. Because we are unfamiliar with it, we hesitate to enter into the new, even though we dislike—even intensely—the old.

The biblical illustration of this human tendency is the

Hebrews' reluctance to leave the wilderness to enter the promised land. Although they had experienced the misery of slavery in Egypt and had followed Moses through the hardships of the wilderness journey to the promised land, when they arrived they became frightened. As one becomes frightened, his imagination goes into negative orbit. The Hebrews' collective fear produced a collective bogey. While flowing with the milk and honey which they desired, the promised land also, they feared, was filled with giants. While Moses pleaded with them to trust in the Lord and enter, they drew back and refused. What followed was the repetition cycle. They wandered in the wilderness for the next 40 years—literally going in circles.

The ancient world into which the Christian Gospel entered, particularly in its Greek philosophical setting, was permeated by the view that life in this world is cyclic—like the seasons—and therefore, going nowhere—essentially meaningless. There was no sense of history since events in time and space were basically meaningless. Since they saw no lines of direction in these events, only circles in endless repetition, they could scarcely conceive of goals or development.

The only way to escape this meaningless existence, according to such teachers as Plato, was to enter the world of the spirit where intelligence and meaning resided. This could be accomplished through meditation and prayer. As one contemplated the world of the spirit, he laid hold of meaning for his own life.

2. Our Secular Trap

Our age has its similarities to the ancient Greek world. We, too, know the despair of going nowhere. Some of our teachers say that our dominant anxiety is that of emptiness and meaninglessness. While we have many things "in the hopper" we wonder, nevertheless, whether anything really changes. In spite of our programs to insure justice for all, many leaders in the fight for racial equality question whether we have made *any* progress at all.

Despite advances in law enforcement, the increase in crime has become an international problem. There are anti-poverty programs galore, but there is evidence to indicate that the poor are actually becoming poorer. Are we simply putting new patches on old garments? Are we only rearranging things rather than changing them? Is it the repetition compulsion at work? If so, the cycle is as follows: pressure is exerted for change; the pressure then diminishes as people get involved in other things, and retrogression begins until soon things are back to where they were—*ad naseum.* There is hope in our day, but it is maintained by a slender thread. It could easily collapse into despair.

In contrast to the culture of the ancient Greeks, however, our age has no spiritual world to which to escape. In short, our society has become secularized. The word "secular" means "of this age—of this world." It is contrasted with "sacred" which means that which transcends this world—the holy. In a former age we made a distinction between the secular and the sacred. Certain activities were called spiritual or religious, and others, secular. We acknowledged the need for both. Now—so far as public life is concerned—it is all secular.

In Dietrich Bonhoeffer's words, ours is the world come of age. As a human society, we are no longer dependent upon a transcendent God. We have grown up—learning to depend on ourselves instead. In Freudian terms, we no longer as a culture have the child-like need to project the father image into the universe and call it God. When we have come of age, we can do without parents, including a Heavenly Parent.

There are, of course, still vestiges of the sacred remaining. We continue to have "In God We Trust" on our coins, and our Congress still opens its sessions with prayer, but these are holdovers from the past. So far as the institutions that dominate our society are concerned—the universities, business and industry, the military, even the government—plans are made and carried out as though God and the sacred did not exist. Such matters, we say, are irrelevant today so far as our technology, our projects and our objectives are concerned.

While our reference has been to the dominant organizations in our society, we as individuals also are greatly affected by this secularization process. Technology and science govern the way we think. We are action-oriented and evaluate in terms of tangible results, productivity, expansion, and the *facts* of sensory perception. For these reasons we are not good meditators. As products of our culture, we have a difficult time in justifying meditation in productive terms. In fact, it may put us behind in our schedule.

Even our churches are not known today for their emphasis on devotional practices. Oriented as we are to the secular, we find it difficult to hold even to the *remnants* of a personal devotional life. Even "saying grace" seems out of place in an age when transcendent values are looked upon as ornamental and quaint rather than relevant.

Obviously this is not a good situation. As children of our culture, we are missing something. The fascination that many young people have today for the eastern religions and practices which emphasize meditation indicates that they feel a lack of something. Even drugs are related to this need. They stimulate the "inner trip" or experience that compensates for inner emptiness.

But we cannot—or should not—return to the days when we divided life into the sacred and secular. Life needs to be integrated, not segmented. As Martin Luther said, our citizenship as Christians is in two worlds, the kingdom on the left hand—the world of human society—and the kingdom on the right hand—the world of the church—of the Spirit. Yet these two should be integrated in the believer's life, since the same God is Lord of both kingdoms. When we are involved in only one of these kingdoms, our needs as a human being are not being met. Our spirit becomes dissatisfied. This is why we use the word "empty." Although society is affluent, our spirits are empty.

The common curse today is boredom. One who is afflicted for any length of time with inactivity or, even worse, with the company of only himself, may refer to the situation as "killing time." In our spiritual emptiness, one of the most precious commodities that we have —time—becomes an enemy. Our hostility toward it is shown in the metaphor of wanting to "kill" it. In ridding ourselves of time, we are wishing for death. Yet our real desire obviously is for life.

The frustration of wanting that which we seemed doomed not to find gives us a feeling of being trapped. All about are walls but no doors, or as John Paul Sartre put it, "no exit." We can go only in the circle of a meaningless and yet painful existence.

One is reminded of the familiar frustration dream in which the dreamer is being pursued—usually by a shadowy figure or power—and cannot seem to get his legs moving. They seem weighted down and move only sluggishly as the pursuer advances. The dream usually ends in panic as the dreamer realizes he is trapped. His predicament is not only one of futility and dissatisfaction. He is in danger of being caught! The reaction is not depression, but anxiety—panic!

Dreams often show what is going on at the feeling level within us. Meaninglessness and emptiness can create anxiety. In fact, we refer to the *anxiety* of meaninglessness and emptiness. It is also the reason the use of drugs is not confined to young people. The tranquilizers and barbiturates used principally by adults are an antidote to anxiety. We are not just trapped, but are fearful of being caught! The low self-image fears the consequences—fears the judgment!

We do not fear simply our own self-judgment. At least in our own awareness we are not both the pursuer and the pursued. As in the dream, we may not even know who or what we dread. Could it be that the transcendent element reënters the scene in this manner? Despite our secularization, we do not seem to have "come of age" in the depths of our anxieties. Here we are not in charge!

How can we change what is destined to repeat itself? A compulsion is by its very nature irresistible, with its "hint of possession by some daemonic power." Are the walls of our entrapment impenetrable? Every wall, said Ralph Waldo Emerson, is a door. This was his expression of faith and hope in that which transcends our secular world. When we feel we are trapped, the situation seems reversed. Every door turns out to be an illusion. To reverse Emerson, every door is a wall! What now can we do?

4. Reacting to Conflict

When faced with being trapped, we can either react or respond. I am differentiating between these terms arbitrarily because I believe it will help us to do so. By *react* I mean that we are so repelled by what we see that we are afraid to come to grips with it. By *respond* I mean that although what we see is frightening, we also see hope, and therefore are able to cope with it. In this chapter we will confine ourselves to ways in which we *react* to conflict.

We will discuss three ways which have been developed by the cultural analyst, Karen Horney. She saw each as a neurotic—or panic—way of reacting to our inner conflicts. We shall develop them from our own point of view as different reactions to the seemingly perpetual conflict between what *is* and what *should be.*

1. *Run from It*

The first way is to run from it. This is perhaps the most common reaction. We run to anything that will distract —anything that will take our attention from the conflict. Maybe this is why people in our society are so terribly busy. We complain about it, but seem afraid of living in any other way. There are those who protest this way of living. Most of these are young people. The majority of us, both youth and adults, are nevertheless caught up in the busy routine and this is therefore one problem that we probably have in common.

Busyness minimizes the pressure of the conflict by displacing it. The busy schedule itself becomes a substitute pressure which we find more tolerable. Whatever awareness we have that we are running—or evading—is counteracted by the pressure to get more pressing things done. Busyness is the justification we need for not confronting what needs to be confronted. It creates addicts known as "workoholics." So long as we are pressed for time, we cannot be bothered with other matters. As a result, the pain of the conflict actually diminishes.

The need to run may account to some extent for the phenomenal popularity and prestige we as a culture give to persons in the entertainment world. Because we need them so badly, we reward them handsomely. Their function is to provide us with persons with whom we can identify and still not know—movie stars, singers, rock artists, sports figures. It is easier to identify with people whom we do not know than people whom we do know. The process is partially fantasy. The entertainers are real people, but our relationship with them is not real. We fill in the gaps with our imagination. We are "in charge." In contrast, when we identify with people whom we know, we may experience tensions that threaten our self-image.

This same tendency also exists in regard to the activities of these entertainers. We get involved as spectators in dramas and athletic contests. We participate only in our imagination. Again this is easier than participating in reality. The drama of our life situation is the most difficult reality of all. The current film scene is an illustration of the hold this substitute involvement has upon young people. Young people virtually are keeping Hollywood in business. This is why the films are directed mostly to youth. Movies are a satisfying medium of entertainment. Yet their great popularity among today's youth, together with the shock effect of their content, strongly indicate that they also are being used to compensate for the lack of an emotionally satisfying involvement with real people in everyday life.

Certainly the desire for escape is also a factor in the phenomenal rise in the use of drugs in our culture. It has been estimated that we spend $150,000,000 a year for three tons of tranquilizers and barbiturates. There are approximately 6,500,000 alcoholics in the United States. Approximately $400,000,000 is spent for the extremely dangerous drug, heroin. The widespread use of LSD, amphetamines and marijuana is common knowledge. We have been called the addictive society because of this large-scale psychological and physical dependence on one or another of these chemical "comforters."

Although drugs vary in their effect, to a greater or lesser degree they create changes in perception within the user. These chemically induced changes provide him with the experience of warmth and harmony that he desires. Under the influence of the drug, the pain of conflict diminishes. The problem with this "solution" is that it is artificial. When the drug's effects wear off, one is back in the same old world. In addition, there is always the danger of developing at least a psychological dependence upon the drug. But the need to run is strong and the many escape routes available in our society make running the easiest way to react to entrapment.

2. Stare at It

In direct contrast to the person who runs from the conflict is the person who stares at it. If we would caricature him, his eyes would be wide open with dark circles under them. He sees only the *is*. The *should* simply mocks the reality of what *is*. The starer is reacting. Though he is facing the conflict, he is demoralized by it. It leaves him chronically depressed, discouraged, defeated. He is immobilized by his distress. Dissatisfied with the way things are, he refuses to be comforted; preoccupied with his pain, he is not distractible. In fact, he has no desire to escape. Being relentlessly realistic, he remains absorbed by the specter of the *is* and overwhelmed by the futility of changing it. Turned inward on himself, he consciously, perhaps even deliberately, absorbs the suffering. Since he feels unable to do anything else, he can at least experience the pain.

I counseled with a girl who reacted this way during her first year at college. She came to see me because she was too depressed to concentrate on her studies. A very sensitive girl, she picked up all the negative innuendoes in any situation. She had hoped things would be different at college, but after a promising beginning, the old patterns began repeating themselves.

"I've been depressed for so long now, it's practically a habit," she said. She did not realize when she said this how significant it was. We *are* creatures of habit. The repetition compulsion is based partially on habit. After a time, we become accustomed to feeling a certain way and subconsciously perpetuate it.

"I wonder what it would be like not to be depressed."

When she said this, I encouraged her to use her imagination. "Numbness," she said, "just numbness. There are times even now when I get so weary of feeling down that I just don't *feel* at all."

Those who stare too long may hurt their eyes, so those who suffer long and futilely from negative feelings may lose their capacity to feel. They may reach what Rollo May calls the "state of feelingness" which he defines as the despairing possibility that nothing matters. Apathy may be the end result of caring very much—but to no avail.

3. *Believing the* Should *is the* Is

A third way of reacting to the conflict between the *should* and the *is*, is to see only the *should*. Those who react in this way find the *is* more of a threat to their self-image than they can tolerate, so they attempt to rid themselves of the *is* by not looking at it. They do so not by distractions, but by deception. Unlike the ostrich which supposedly puts its head in the sand so it cannot see the *is*, these reactors put their heads in the direction of the *should*. By so doing, they attempt to convince themselves that the *should* is the *is*.

Obviously the procedure is a ruse. By closing his eyes to the spirit—his feelings and motives—and concentrating only on forms, the person who reacts in this way hopes the contradictions will go away. Since he cannot control his feelings and motives, he concentrates on his external behavior. This creates for him the illusion that what he wants to believe about himself is so. The *should* is the *is*.

The *is* does not so easily disappear. Whenever it threatens to come into his range of vision, he begins to feel uncomfortable. Defensively he rationalizes the threat away before it can destroy his ruse. In counseling, however, this is difficult to do. The counselor has a way of exposing these rationalizations.

"I shouldn't feel this way," the counselee says, ready to drop the matter. "Let's put the *should* aside for the time being," says the counselor, "and concentrate on what *is*— how you feel, not on how you *should* feel." The counselee may be frightened at such a prospect, but also relieved. Evidently the counselor can accept him where he *is* rather than where he *should* be.

Should he continue to reject the *is*, however, he will become an increasingly divided person. The success of the evasion depends on his ability to deceive himself. Should anyone want evidence of the complexity of human nature, let him contemplate the fact that a human being can deceive *himself*—that he can be both the deceiver and the deceived. Fortunately, the process is not foolproof. The inner life we would like to hide, even from ourselves, with its unacceptable feelings, thoughts, motives, emptiness, as well as its intractable jealousies, fantasies, hostilities, envies, weaknesses, is in constant danger of exposure. The external facade—the image of ourselves we try to cultivate as unselfish, friendly, cool—is not always convincing. Yet the success of the deception depends upon keeping this contrast between the external and the internal out of sight, out of consciousness.

The price one pays for his success is that he becomes a stranger to himself. He cannot afford to know what is going on within himself. Otherwise he would see the contrast to his projected image and his defenses would collapse. To maintain the substitution of the *should* for the *is*, he must sacrifice his opportunity to know who he is.

As previously indicated, this is not entirely successful.

The *is* does not disappear. Rather, it remains as our darker side which haunts the distortedly positive self-image. Psychoanalyst Carl Jung identifies these two sides of our person as the ego image and its shadow. The ego image is the image of what we should be and have convinced ourselves and others that we are. The shadow is the ego image's contradiction, its opposite. They are the twin distortions, positively and negatively, of who we are. The success of the endeavor depends upon keeping them apart.

Although he is persona-non-grata, the shadow continually threatens to emerge into sight. To survive, the ego image must prevent this emergence. Yet it cannot do so completely. The shadow comes out in indirect ways which are not easily recognized. One of the most common targets for the shadow's projection is another person with similar characteristics. To ensure projection, the projector may launch a self-righteous attack on his victim.

This tendency to project our shadow onto others is a factor in the polarization of our society. It is particularly obvious in the racial polarization. It is also a frequent phenomenon in intimate relationships between husbands and wives, parents and children, brothers and sisters with each other, and friends with friends.

To avoid a confrontation with our shadow, we have to resort to dishonesty. Because of the widespread use of this particular way of reacting, we are currently experiencing an honesty "kick" in compensation. This is the impetus behind the popularity of sensitivity groups. These groups provide an atmosphere of acceptance for the *is*. In this milieu one can be honest in what he says and does. The extremes to which some of these groups may go in ridding persons of their barriers only show how bottled up and blocked many of these people are.

The result of these and other contemporary expressions

of liberation is that honesty has become the popular virtue. Who can but rejoice in any appreciation for honesty? Yet an honesty *binge* has within it the potential for the very evils it purports to counteract. Whenever we exalt one virtue above others, we tend to become moralistic about it. We assume we demonstrate it by talking about it and expressing it. These assumptions lay the groundwork for another ego image in which the *should*, "honesty," is substituted for the *is*. What then to do with the shadow, the *is?* Project it upon others—those in whom we see the shadow characteristics of dishonesty! Flay the hypocrites! "At least I'm honest!" we say. Are we? Or is this simply a way of reacting to the *is?* We can almost hear the refrain, "God I thank thee that I am not like these hypocrites!"

These three ways of reacting to the conflict between the *should* and the *is*—running, staring and projecting—are not exhaustive. They are, however, representative. Though diverse, they each depend upon the same repugnance toward the *is* and the same feelings of impotence toward coping positively and directly with it. As a result, the basic conflict not only remains but becomes even more destructive.

Before we discuss more healthy ways of approaching the problem, we need to investigate another obstacle in our way. We not only fear what we see; we are made to feel guilty by it, also. This further complicates the problem and its possible solution.

5. The Drive to Self-Sacrifice

In each of the three ways of reacting to the contrast between the *should* and the *is*—running from it, staring at it, and believing the *should* is the *is*—the reactor is being affected in one way or another by what Karen Horney calls the "tyranny of the should." The vision of the *should,* instead of being an incentive for growth, so tyrannizes a person's conscience that he becomes unable to act. He remains in an unproductive state of self-judgment. This may occur even when he seems to have no conscience problems.

Conscience is indigenous to human nature. One cannot eliminate it by ignoring it or by flaunting it. Because a person escapes the familiar problems of guilt, he may be under the illusion that he has no guilt. If conscience problems are not dealt with directly, they manifest themselves indirectly. In ways we scarcely recognize as conscience repercussions, we hurt and destroy ourselves; we sabotage our opportunities to receive or to achieve what supposedly we want.

1. *The Need to Punish Ourselves*

While we may not recognize these destructive tendencies as symptoms of a conscience tyrannized by the *should,* the effects provide the evidence. We are punishing ourselves. The inner emptiness that plagues us is an expression of how worthless we feel. These misgivings about our own worth carry with them little hope of fulfilling our aspirations. The low self-image limits our productivity. It will not let us receive—either from others or from our own efforts—more than we deserve. Since the self-image is low, its projected level of deserving is also low.

Some of us have a need for self-punishment. Bob is an example. Although he has the potential for achievement, he never feels that anything he does is good enough. Rather than feeling good about what he has accomplished, he feels badly about what he still has not achieved. He is most uncomfortable when complimented, and feels compelled to disparage the compliment. Most of the anger that he experiences is directed toward himself. At these times he berates himself severely. Yet even when he feels anger toward somebody else, he holds it inside. There it creates discomfort primarily for himself.

Occasionally when with others, Bob may discover that he is actually enjoying himself. Almost immediately he feels guilty for feeling so good. As a reaction, he conjures up something to stew about—some fear or doubt or failure—and thereby destroys his momentary enjoyment—his peace.

What is Bob's problem? It would seem that he is always trying to make up for, or making an *atonement* for what he is not. This means that he thinks very little of himself—that he has little self-esteem. In moments of somber reflection, he wonders if others could really love him if they could see him as he sees himself. Quite obviously he does not like himself.

Bob's need for self-punishment is a detriment to his intimate relationships. His relationship with his girlfriend is a case in point. If she pays even passing attention to other fellows, Bob's low self-image reacts. Feeling threatened by even the hint of competition, he becomes jealous. As would be expected, he does not voice his feelings directly. Instead, he becomes sullen, uncommunicative. The same thing happens if his girlfriend criticizes him. To Bob criticism is tantamount to rejection. Since his imperfections constitute the basis for his self-rejection, it is understandable that his girlfriend's criticisms—even though offered constructively—would simply magnify these imperfections. He becomes angry, but instead of expressing his feelings, he withdraws into silence. The more she tries to draw him out, the more he withdraws into himself. He obviously is punishing her. Yet he is also punishing himself.

Jim is self-destructive, also, but in a different way. In contrast to Bob, he "acts out" rather than "in." He will try anything for a dare. Although he has fears like anybody else, his best defense against them is a good offense. Instead of withdrawing to safety, he attacks his fears through dare-devil antics. Jim flares easily. Instead of keeping his anger within, he attacks the immediate object of his wrath. Obviously he gets into quite a few scrapes.

While his life is full of activity, the activities frequently are destructive, even to his own interests. Being impulsive, he seems to have a knack for sabotaging his opportunities. As an example, he has lost three jobs either due to "goofing off" or to fights. His problem goes deeper than his emotional impulsiveness. Why is he impulsive?

Jim finds it very painful to look at himself. In contrast to Bob, he does not turn inward. He finds it too disconcerting. What little he sees gets him keyed up and restless. Consequently he needs strong external distractions. He calls these by the right word: "I'm the kind of guy that needs lots of *excitement.*" He has to have it.

Because of the impetus behind them, Jim's exciting distractions, also take on the character of self-sabotage. He does not like to look inward because his self-image is low. In acting out his negative feelings in exciting and often destructive escapades, he evades any real involvement with his own person. Yet these reactions to his unacknowledged guilt continue. Although he does not realize it, Jim is anything but free. Behind the restlessness that drives him to seek excitement are the inescapable reverberations from his low sense of worth.

2. Religious Overtones

The need for punishment has religious overtones. Among ancient peoples this need was met by offering some kind of sacrifice to the god or gods to whom they felt obligated. The religion of the ancient Hebrews is our prime example. The books of the Old Testament did not institute the sacrificial system but rather codified what was already an established practice. Much of the content of two of these books, Leviticus and Deuteronomy, concerns these regulations of the cultic sacrifice.

Sacrifices were offered regularly, first at the tabernacle and later at the temple, by a traditionally constituted priesthood. The sacrifices were of three sorts: the daily burnt offerings, the daily meal offerings and the sin offerings at each new moon, at the religious festivals, and especially at the Day of Atonement, Yom Kippur. It is these sin offerings that pertain to the need for punishment.

The sacrifices for the sin offerings were animals: a

young bull, a goat, or a lamb. Besides the regularly stated occasions, these sacrifices were offered by the priests at other times on behalf of specific individuals under the immediate judgment of sin. The most important sin offering, however, was offered annually on the Day of Atonement. Observed as a solemn fast day by the people, the ritual of the Day of Atonement took place in the temple. The high priest alone entered the Holy of Holies, the third and inmost court or curtained area of the temple. Following the ritual, he slew a young bull, a goat, and a ram and offered them upon the altar. Another goat called the scapegoat or *escape* goat was driven into the wilderness to die after the high priest symbolically laid upon it the sins of the people. In these ways he offered an atonement for his own sins, for the sins of his people, and for the alleviation of their guilt.

Obviously the sacrificial system belongs to a primitive and agrarian people. Though it may still be continued among some primitive tribes, it has no meaning for a modern industrialized culture. Who would want to revive it? Even the Israelites prefer their present modifications of the ancient practices to a reinstitution of these practices. As repugnant as it may be to modern man, however, the sacrificial system is still a more sensible approach to the problem of the low self-image than our current modes of offering *ourselves*.

Among the Hebrews human sacrifice was condemned. The neighboring peoples practiced human sacrifice. For this and other reasons the Hebrews were warned by their leaders not to consort with them. Now as "civilized people" we again have the problem of human sacrifice, not literally or ceremonially, of course, but nonetheless effective. Through our self-destructive tendencies we surely, even though slowly, undermine our opportunities, destroy our satisfactions, block our development.

Believing that this self-destructive tendency observed in human beings was related to the process of death inherent in nature, Freud called it a "death instinct." The need to punish ourselves drives us into activities related more to death and destruction than to life and growth. Though the primitive awareness of this need has dimmed in our industrial age, the need itself continues to influence our behavior.

The animal sacrifice system for alleviating guilt is dated to the culture of its day. It cannot be revived even if we would desire to do so. Our hope is for a better way, a way more relevant to our day and to our needs. Even in its own day the sacrificial system had its built-in limitations, its serious shortcomings. Yet our own self-destructiveness is far more limiting. Our hope is for a better way than either of these.

For those who so hope, there is Good News. There *is* a better way. Before we look into it, however, we need to understand more fully the purpose for the punishment. Why should people feel moved to so inflict themselves? Is it completely self-destructive? Or are there advantages—enlightened self-interest advantages—in punishing ourselves?

6. Forestalling the Greater Punishment

Behavior that appears self-destructive is rarely completely so. The extreme in self-destruction, suicide, may seem to be the exception. Yet even suicide is more complicated than it appears. When one reaches the distortion in reasoning that precedes suicide, he actually sees advantages to taking his life. If nothing more, he longs for an end to his mental torment. In fact, the fear of *eternal* punishment has been a deterrent to suicide. In a former day when our views of suicide were more simplistic and our belief in hell more literally fire-and-brimstone, suicide was considered a sure route to everlasting punishment. No matter how miserable one was, the thought of hell seemed worse.

With the lessening of this fear, the advantages in suicide to the distorted mind are more pronounced. In addition to the cessation of torment, there is the satisfaction of bringing pain and guilt to those with whom one is angry. In some instances suicide also offers the advantage of avoiding public disgrace.

If there are advantages even in suicide to the distorted reason, there obviously are advantages in punishing oneself less drastically that would appeal to a less distorted mind. Such a person would seek these advantages in life rather than in death. He is not simply driven by guilt, which is symbolic of the past; he is also pulled by desire which is symbolic of the future. Even in self-punishment he seeks something which would be to his advantage. There is a purpose to it, not just a cause.

1. Protection Against the Consequences of Guilt

Self-punishment is not an end in itself. The destruction it brings is not for its own sake. Self-punishment is a *means*—a means for achieving a goal. Obviously the goal has sufficient pull to compensate for the self-inflicted pain required to obtain it.

Punishment, even in its abstract definition, is not simply the suffering inflicted upon a person guilty of wrong. Rather, its intention is to provide a learning experience from which he and perhaps others may benefit. Ideally speaking, this is the intention behind parental punishment —often called parental *discipline*, which means providing a learning experience. Of course we know that punishment can be exploited by parents as well as other authority figures to satisfy their own distorted needs. So widespread is this exploitation that psychiatrist Karl Menninger has written a book about it with the ominous title, *The Crime of Punishment*.

A symbol of this *crime* is what physicians call "the battered child syndrome." The increasing number of helpless children who are cruelly beaten by their parents is cause for alarm. Ironically, those who commit such a crime usually justify it as a corrective. "I did it to make him mind," says the guilty parent.

This situation has also occurred in our treatment of criminals. The "corrective" may become an even worse crime than the original breach of the law. Authorities who are filled with hostility find a "justified" outlet for it in the unlucky offender. Since society has labeled him an offender, it is less concerned about his rights as a human being.

Ideally, however, punishment is protective. Though harsh at times, its purpose is to protect one from something even harsher. For example, parental discipline reflects the discipline inherent in life. Today certain parental education theories stress permitting a child to experience the natural and logical consequences of his behavior to effect discipline rather than punishment. However, the essential point is that the child who absorbs this discipline at home is in a better position to leave home. Even the criminal is supposedly incarcerated in order that he might become rehabilitated or at least be given protective confinement.

The same is true of self-punishment. As distorted as it may be, its purpose is to protect ourselves against a greater punishment. What is this greater punishment? Though its form is vague, it is the dreaded consequences of our guilt. In punishing ourselves we are trying to stave off this "judgment" by executing it ourselves.

When I was a child, I seemed to get my share of splinters. On each occasion my father would get out the needle, sterilize it in boiling water, and take out my splinter. I dreaded these times. I did not doubt their necessity, but I longed for the day when I could do it myself. I wanted to take the needle into my own hands.

When the time finally came that I could do this myself, I made a bloodier mess of extracting my splinter than my father ever had made, and I had more pain by far than when my father held the needle, but I *felt good*—because *I* was in control of the needle. Despite the blood and the pain I had no intention of returning to the former situa-

tion. The amount of suffering was not the issue—it was
my control over it. I had less anxiety, even though I had
more pain. In fact, anxiety was the *greater* pain.

During the Middle Ages there were people called *flag-
ellants* because they flagellated (whipped) themselves.
They were religious people—Christians—and their volun-
tary flagellation was a religious rite. The practice began
in the eleventh century and continued at sporadic inter-
vals until the early part of the nineteenth century. Beginning as a new form of devotion in the monasteries of
western Europe, especially among the Franciscans, the practice was contagious and spread as a spontaneous popular
movement throughout Europe. Long processions could
be seen regularly on country roads and city streets—people
of all ages and classes reciting prayers and whipping themselves with long leather thongs until the blood flowed
from their bodies. Though their bodies smarted with pain
and their skin was flayed into ribbons, they felt good—
they felt cleansed. Flagellation had become a way of sal-
vation.

If we would beat ourselves in this way today—at least
publically—we would be considered mentally unbalanced
and confined to the safeguards of a mental hospital. Yet
we beat ourselves up in other ways which are not so
socially offensive. Mentally, emotionally, personally, we
flagellate ourselves to secure our desired ends. In our self-
destructive bent we undermine our friendships, destroy our
intimate relationships, impair our vocation and sabotage our achievements.

Such actions would seem to be nothing but a binge in
self-sabotage. Yet in reality they are *purposeful* activities.
Regardless of what we seem to be losing, we are protecting ourselves against the fear of a greater loss. As long as

we do our own sabotaging, we have not lost control over the judgment we fear. Should we lose this control, we would be forced to enter into the anxiety of the unknown, where one awaits the fateful strike, not knowing when or how.

2. Need for Control of Punishment

We have a need to remain in control of the punishment we feel we deserve. Though it stems from the conscience, this is not simply a religious need. Atheists as well as believers have it. Guilt goes with being human. Religion has no corner on the conscience. Though they do not express them in the traditional religious categories, non-religious persons also have their problems with their conscience. The mental imagery by which they perceive these problems is obviously different, but the emotional dynamics and functional rationale are similar.

The similarity may also be seen from the opposite direction. Religion may prevent rather than cause disturbance of conscience. Terrible things have been done in defense of religion. During the inquisition, Catholics put other Christians to torture and death for heresy. During the witch trials in Puritan New England, Protestants put other Christians to torture and death on suspicion of being "witches." We might take satisfaction from the fact that these events took place centuries ago, except for the contemporary fact that some Protestants and some Catholics in Northern Ireland hate each other enough to burn, bomb and shoot each other in their so-called "religious" war.

When hatred of this sort is fostered in the name of religion, the shadowing side of human nature has been projected onto an enemy. The punishment which the shadow deserves is meted out to another. The "enemy," then, is the victim of a displaced hostility: we elected to punish *him* for *our* guilt. The ruse depends upon how completely one is able to identify himself with his ego image and his victim with its shadow. The conflict, then, is between the good guys and the bad guys, with the solution dependent upon the destruction of the bad guys. If the good guys are shown to have any of the bad guys' qualities, and the bad guys are shown to have any of the good guys' qualities, the "jig is up." Then we are left with the more odious task of punishing *ourselves*.

Whether religious or non-religious, the rationale for wanting to remain in control of the punishment is the same. It is as though one were to say to God—or whatever powers there be—"Look, I know I don't deserve very much, so I'll take the responsibility of seeing that I don't get more. In fact, I'll see that I get less than I deserve, just to reassure you that things are under control and there is no need for you to intervene!" This is the bookkeeping system for maintaining the peace. Debits and credits must be kept in balance. If we go "into the red," that is, have more good fortune than our conscience can tolerate, we go into debt. Consequently we need to add more credits to restore the peace or balance. Just to insure it, we may throw in a few extra credits—pains, deprivations, failures.

In this bookkeeping system the conscience indicates the state of balance. According to St. Paul, our conscience "bears witness" to where we stand, while our "conflicting thoughts" either accuse or excuse us. Though it is a distinctly human faculty, conscience takes on transcendental dimensions. It is projected into the universe as a cosmic witness. Whether we call this projection *God* or simply *act* as though it was God, the result is the same. Sacrifices must be offered to pacify this witness. No substitutes, however, are permitted: only our own "blood" can suffice.

Since the system depends upon having more payments or credits than are strictly necessary, the "bloodier" the sacrifice, the more stable is the balance—the peace. So long as the magnified conscience remains dominant, the punishment we administer to ourselves—or to the victims of our projected shadow—forestalls the Greater Punishment, whose nebulous form is forever threatening to emerge from the dim edges of consciousness.

3. *Distortion of Freedom*

Strange as it may seem, this need to maintain control of the punishment we feel we deserve is a manifestation of human freedom. Because it stems from alienation, however, it is a negative use of freedom, arising from a phobia over dependence. If one has trouble trusting others, he may fear being destroyed should he come under their control. This lack of trust extends also to the universe—to God. There is a desperate resistance, consequently, to surrendering any control over our needs to others.

One would naturally expect some such resistance to dependence among young people seeking emancipation from their parents. Since growing up usually is accompanied by some degree of rebellion, I would imagine that you also feel strongly attracted to independence. This is a normal reaction to a long period of dependence. When this reaction has run its course, most of us settle for *inter*dependence. We realize that as persons who live together in communities, we have needs that depend upon others for their satisfaction. This is the cohesive force in group living—from the family to society at large. Our relationships are held intact by the exchange of mutual needs and satisfactions. In mutual dependence—interdependence—there is also freedom.

In the meantime one can get *hung up* on independence. Because of his negative attitude toward dependence, he may be attracted to its opposite in his quest for freedom. It is an old myth, extending back as far as the Garden of Eden. Why did Adam and Eve eat of the forbidden fruit? Because they hoped to escape their position of dependence. The tempter knew where to make his pitch. "For God knows that when you eat of it your eyes will be opened, and you will be like God, knowing good and evil." (Gen. 3:5). Being *like* God is different from being *under* God, even as having one's own knowledge is something other than trusting in God. Yet the damage to relationships that followed indicates the distortion in that choice.

The more we fear dependence, the more we are compelled to be free of it. Note the contradiction in terms. If one is *compelled*, he is no longer free. He flees one servitude only to enter into another. In his quest for freedom, he finds himself in even deeper bondage.

Yet there may be a legitimate basis for this fear of dependence. Whenever one individual has control over another, he has power over him. Under the corrupting influence of power, he may be tempted to exploit the dependent one. He may—as we say—take advantage of him.

One need not be unkind to be exploitive. The most subtle exploitations are difficult to discern because they function under the aura of kindness. The giving of a compliment is one for example. A well-known guide for management instructs employers in the use of the compliment as a means for increasing the productivity of the employee. It stresses that the compliment be sincere. Yet how can it be sincere if one is using it to his own advantage? The victims of these subtle forms of manipulation may suspect that even an honest compliment stems from ulterior motives. "What's his angle?" they ask. They fear being *used*—being "taken."

One of my students had this suspicion of teachers. Since she was not doing well in her studies, she made an appointment for counseling. I offered a few suggestions and in the next test she received an A. As I returned her paper, I complimented her: "Keep up the good work!" I still recall the way in which she looked at me. In the next test she received an F. Being nonplussed, I asked her to explain. "You thought you could control me by complimenting me," she said, "and I was not going to give you that satisfaction." This girl was willing to "cut off her nose to spite her face," an example of the length to which some persons may go when freedom becomes a compulsion. It is the freedom, then, only to destroy.

The most unforgetable example of this destructive use of freedom is that of a man who had a long history of self-destruction. The trend began in earnest when he went to college. Being a gifted person, he did well academically. His parents were proud of this and boasted about him to relatives and neighbors. He resented this as an exploitation for their own needs. Yet he could not tell them directly how he felt. Instead he began to goof off in his studies and subsequently he flunked out. Now he was no longer exploitable. He enlisted in the armed services and became a candidate for officer training. His parents again were thrilled. Once more they told the relatives and neighbors. Once more, also, the young man did a slow burn. Before receiving his commission, he became involved in a brawl with his commanding officer and was disqualified.

Returning home from service, he married and went to work for a large corporation. He was encouraged by his boss to train for a junior executive position. His parents' hopes were revived. Relatives and friends again were notified. By now they should have suspected a repeat. It was not long in coming. After quarreling violently with a fellow employee, the man demanded that his boss take his part. When the boss was reluctant to do so, he quit his job.

What more could he still sabotage? Unfortunately his parents were pleased with his marriage. He had "married well," as they put it, and they boasted to the relatives and neighbors about it. How could the young man stop *this?* He picked the surest way—he began to run around with other women. Unable to penetrate his compulsion to destroy, his wife sued for divorce. Once again he had succeeded.

In the loneliness that followed, he began to realize that in sabotaging his parents' pride, he had undermined his own fulfillment. Fortunately—or unfortunately—he loved his wife. Like the prodigal son in the Bible, he "came to himself." In the hope of reëstablishing his marriage, he sought out help.

The resistance to domination can become as binding as the conformity one seeks to escape. It is slavery in the opposite direction. The man with the history of self-sabotage had an exaggerated need to free himself from the exploitation of his parents. Ultimately, only self-destruction could satisfy this need. We can become so hypersensitive to any invasion of our freedom that our defense against it becomes suicidal in nature. Suicide itself, as Rollo May points out, is the ultimate act a person can make as an assertion of his power—his independence. It is the tragic culmination of the negative use of freedom.

In most instances we are not fully aware of the self-destructiveness of our actions. The impulsive way in which we frequently act makes it difficult to discern the complexity of our motivation, particularly when this motivation involves something as unflattering as self-punishment. Then the defensive impulse to rationalize may take over. How, then, can you know when you are caught in this cycle of self-sabotage?

You may penetrate to some extent your rationalizations by asking yourself in all honesty how you feel about yourself. Keep the question before you, even though it makes you uncomfortable. If you need help in finding an answer, imagine yourself in the presence of God—or the projected image of your conscience. Now—how do you feel? The answer to this question tells you a lot about yourself—and your God. Our actions are directly related to our self-image, even though we may not be aware of the connection. Consequently it is important that this self-image be positive. We turn now to the Good News about how this can be possible.

7. Good News

The agonizing aspect of the gap between the *should* and the *is,* is our inability to bridge it.

We are overcome by the weight of our own impotency. This impotency shows up clearly in the data from surveys of the Youth Research Center headquartered in Minneapolis. For example, in the center's latest survey of young people, 13 descriptions of a lack in self-confidence were listed. The expression, "things sometimes do not go the way I want them to," had the smallest number of denials. Only 6 percent of the 6,000 youth tested indicated they were not bothered by this recurring frustration. Of even more significance, the category of response, "no longer bothered" had by far the lowest number of all responses to these problems in confidence. Only an average of 5 percent were consciously aware of any progress in any of these personal frustrations.

The opposite of impotency is, of course, power. We hear much about power today. There is black power, red power, brown power and student power. Martin Luther King's initial reaction to the slogan, "black power," was skepticism. To him, the demand for power was in contrast to his emphasis on love and non-violence.

The idea of power has long been viewed with suspicion because of the repeated destruction brought about by the *lust* for power. "Power corrupts," said Lord Acton, "and absolute power corrupts absolutely." Yet power is also a legitimate resource in human activity. Like other resources, it is ours to use. The moral aspect does not concern power itself but how it is used. Atomic power and sexual power, for example, are capable of great destruction or great blessing.

Our use of power is a matter of stewardship, even as is our use of money, time, and other possessions. A steward is one appointed by a master to oversee the use of the master's goods. We are responsible to God for what we do with the resources he has made available to us. As an escape from this responsibility, some of us may be like the steward in Jesus' parable who buried the money allotted to him in the ground to prevent its being lost. Rather than being commended by his master, he was rebuked, because money is to use, not to bury. So also power.

1. *Power to Break the Repetition Compulsion*

First we need to ask whether there is such a power—a power to break the repetition compulsion. Any affirmative answer would be good news. Consequently, it is no coincidence that this power actually is called Good News. The Biblical word *Gospel* is a contraction of what was originally "Good Spell" (news). The Good News is that there is such a power and the power itself comes through the Good News. Is this Good News, then, simply a message? It is a message that brings about a relationship with God and this, in turn, affects our relationship with our self and our neighbor. As such, it calls into being a communion of believers. The Good News is the Good News of *Christ*.

There are many descriptive names for Christ—all of

them attempt to communicate who he is. The name "Jesus" itself is a given name meaning "Jehovah Saves." The term "Christ" is a title—"Jesus, the Christ"—meaning "God's Anointed One." It is the Greek word for the Hebrew, Messiah. Anointing with oil was the ceremonial way of setting a person apart for a special task.

Some names refer to the nature of his being: Son of man, Son of God, Emanuel. Others refer to his function: Redeemer, Savior, Mediator, Prince of Peace, Lord of Lords and King of Kings, the Teacher, the Prophet, the Great High Priest. Still others refer to what he reveals: He is the Way, the Truth, the Life, the Light of the world. "He that has seen me," he said, "has seen the Father" (John 14:9).

As the Revealer, he is not the projected image of our conscience. This would *not* be good news. Rather, his function is to emancipate us from the hold of this projected image. This *is* good news. He quoted the words of the Old Testament prophet as referring to himself: "The Spirit of the Lord God is upon me because the Lord has anointed me to bring good news to the afflicted, he has sent me to bind up the broken hearted, to proclaim liberty to the captives, and the opening of the prison to those who are bound." (Isaiah 61:1).

The projected image of the conscience is a distorted image of God. In contrast, there is the truth about God which, Christ said, can make us free, for the truth about God is also the truth about man—about ourself. In the person of Christ the transcendent becomes explicit in the immanent. He is *Emanuel*, which means God-with-us. He becomes one of us in order to do for us what we could not do for ourselves. This is the Christmas story. It was he who could make the atonement for us because he was one with us and one with God. He could offer himself as mediator.

As we have noted, the Old Testament priests offered their sacrifices repeatedly. Even the Day of Atonement was an annual affair. Being a Hebrew, Jesus shared in this sacrificial system as a part of his own tradition. Yet unlike that of the Old Testament priests, his offering was not repeated. As the New Testament says, he was offered *once* to bear the sins of many. (Heb. 9:28).

This offering took place as an execution. On a hill called Calvary, Christ was put to death on a cross. His was the supreme sacrifice—unto death. He *was* crucified, that is, he did not crucify himself. He was no masochist. By compromising in his convictions or by fleeing Jerusalem, he could have avoided this fate. If he persisted in his witness to the truth about God, which in turn witnessed to the truth about man, his death was unavoidable. He attacked the political and religious establishment (in Israel they were closely associated) because he considered them corrupt. "You are like whitewashed tombs," he said to these leaders. Though outwardly they appeared beautiful, inwardly they were "full of dead men's bones and all uncleanness." (Matt. 23:27). In the attempt to hold to their traditions, Jesus charged that they had muted the Word of God. "You hypocrites!" he said, "Well did Isaiah prophesy of you, when he said, 'This people honors me with their lips, but their heart is far from me.'" (Matt. 15:7-8).

If the leaders were to remain in power, they had to silence him. Like the long line of prophets that preceded him, he met the violent resistance of the established order. "Which of the prophets did not your fathers persecute?" (Acts 7:52). Yet he was more than a prophet. As he implied in his own parable, he was the Son of God. Even though God's previous messengers had been abused, surely his Son would be respected. Not so. For him they reserved the worst. "This is the heir; come let us kill him and have his inheritance" (Matt. 21:38).

Perhaps you have seen a picture of Jesus on a caricatured "wanted-man" poster that has been circulating about. Accompanying the picture are these words: "Reward for information leading to the apprehension of Jesus Christ, wanted for sedition, criminal anarchy, vagrancy, and conspiring to overthrow the established government. Dresses poor. *Said* to be a carpenter by trade, ill-nourished, has visionary ideas, associates with common working people, the unemployed and bums. Alien—believed to be a Jew. Alias: 'Prince of Peace,' 'Son of Man,' 'Light of the World,' etc., etc. *Professional agitator*, red beard, marks on hands and feet the result of injuries inflicted by an angry mob led by respectable citizens and legal authorities."

Though Jesus did not end the cycle of persecution, he ended the cycle of defeat. He rose from the dead—never to die again. "Death no longer has dominion over him" (Rom. 6:9). He broke the repetition compulsion. He was offered *once*. After this there was nothing more his opponents could do. His death was the overcoming of death. "Death," says St. Paul, "is swallowed up in victory!" (I Cor. 15:54). The victory is the empty tomb. This is the Easter story. It is still best expressed by the ancient Easter greeting, "He is risen: he is risen indeed!"

2. *Power Through Reconciliation*

The gap between the *is* and the *should* in our individual lives obviously has a built-in resistance to closing. The unusually small percentage in the youth survey who had experienced any sense of progress in dealing with their personal shortcomings unfortunately seems to be more typical than not. This resistance to growth is itself a power—one that binds us to our past and predisposes us to the repetition compulsion. This power is our guilt. Whether it is sharply focused or diffused, or simply an impression, the low self-image perpetuates its own existence by predisposing our behavior. The result is a sense of futility based upon a back-log of supporting evidence, namely, repetitive failure.

The Good News concerns the power to break these chains. This power comes into being when we become reconciled to our past. The Good News is that God cares —he cares enough about us to become one of us, to identify with us in our bondage, or, as the New Testament puts it, to be tempted in every respect as we are (Heb. 4:15). God not only cares, he understands. Only he could make the atonement—and he did. In the words of Paul, "God was in Christ reconciling the world to himself." Therefore, he appeals, "be reconciled to God" (II Cor. 5: 19–20).

The Good News is that God loves you in the *is*—in *your is*. The projected-conscience-image says he loves you only in the *should*. The Good News exposes this distortion. When you see yourself as selfish, incompetent, insincere, worthless, phony, perverted, distorted, or as *blah* —there it is that God loves you. He breaks through the barriers of our distorted projections of who he is—and who we are, to reveal himself as he really is—Good News.

God loves you in the *is*. Let him! Let him love you unconditionally. Atonement has been made. Trust him!

When you allow him to love you in the *is, as you are*— you will discover that you can love yourself in the *is*. The

Good News breaks down our own "conditions." Be reconciled to yourself, as you are. Embrace yourself as God has embraced you in Christ. The power to overcome the *is* begins in reconciliation with the *is*. This is the power that breaks the cycle. Something new is added, namely, unconditional love. This is the power that frees us from the bondage to futility into which our own conditions and requirements had placed us. Because these conditions governing our worth only condemned us, we were without the means to face up to them. The Good News removes these conditions. The repetition of the old, consequently, is broken. "Therefore, if any one is in Christ, he is a new creation" (II Cor. 5:17).

3. *Time as Quality*

In the Greek language of the New Testament, two words for time are used: *chronos* and *kairos*. Although the words are at times used interchangeably, at other times they are distinguished in emphasis. *Chronos* is time as *quantity*. It can be measured by a linear standard in terms of seconds, minutes, hours, days, weeks, months, years, centuries, millenia. There are 52 weeks in a year, four weeks in a month, 12 months in a year, so that we can use numbers to define where we are in time. From *chronos* we get the word "chronology," which is the science of measuring time, of dating events and arranging them in order of occurrence.

Kairos is time as *quality*. Its measurement is not by the clock or the calendar. It is evaluated rather than measured and the standards are more subjective than objective. The crucial issue is not *when* but *what*.

In the English language we differentiate time in this

same manner, but use the one word to express each. We say, "I had a good time," or, "This is a great time to be alive." Obviously this is time as quality. The point is not how long or how short is the time, but the quality of our experience of it. In contrast, time as quantity is predetermined by the system of measurement. It is based on the certainty of repetition. Quality or meaning does not enter the picture.

On the other hand, time as quality is anything but predetermined. Meaning, not measurement, is of the essence, as time is emancipated from repetition. Something new can enter into it and seemingly change its pace. "Where did the time go?" we say after an enjoyable experience. Although the chronological measurement was constant, the time *seemed* shorter. Its quality was good. On the other hand, we also say, "That was the longest five minutes of my life." The measurement was constant, but subjectively the meaning was frightening. Or again, "This day seems like it will never end." The sun, of course, has not stopped in its tracks; it just *seems* that way. The quality of time being poor, the experience is boring. Interestingly enough in modern Greek, *chronos* has come to mean year and *kairos*, weather. *Chronos* is still a matter of duration and *kairos* of change.

The Good News centers in time as quality. "When the time (*chronos*) had fully come, God sent forth his Son, born of a woman, born under the law" (Gal. 4:4). An event in time brings meaning to many. The Good News entered into history—*kairos* into *chronos*—so that every moment in *chronos* is also a potential *kairos*. Through the reconciling power of Christ, there is the possibility in each moment for something new. With God's help, and our response, things can change and change for the better.

God's help is available. This is the Good News. Our reception of his help is a different matter. It depends upon our openness to receive. When we are predisposed by the past to defeat and futility, we are not open, but when we become reconciled with this past—can embrace it—we become open.

Our response is not only our openness, but our taking hold. Response comes from the same root as the word responsibility. Our response is our exercise of *responsibil*-ity. God's help increases our own productivity. He gives in ways that stimulate personal responsibility. Those who receive are also to give. Being integrated by his reconciling power, we can *do* what before we could not.

The situation is similar in the challenge to effect change in our society. People have discovered that by organizing together and working hard, they can accomplish things. Minority groups in particular have learned this. From the successful bus boycott in Montgomery, Alabama, in the early 1960's, to the grape pickers' contracts in 1970, many apparently impregnable traditions based on prejudice have given way under the pressures for change. When this happens, the hopes of oppressed people become justified. They lose their sense of futility, grow more confident of their worth, and feel more like free people than prisoners.

We may not always see this change. In fact, we may grow discouraged because we see it so rarely. I wonder how often Cesar Chavez felt discouraged during the many years of effort before he finally secured his contracts with the grape growers. Perhaps you feel similarly discouraged in regard to your personal life. Perhaps you have known the Good News and experienced God's reconciling love, and yet see little, if any, change in your life—little, if any, power.

Change can take place! Yet *seeing* change is not the same as change itself. As the New Testament says, "We walk not by *sight* but by *faith*" (II Cor. 5:7). You can be going somewhere when it seems to you that you are going nowhere. Yet you still may be moving ahead. As Job's counselor, Elihu, said, "God works in one way or in two, though man does not perceive it." God's activity does not depend upon our perception of it. Believing this is walking by faith in contrast to sight.

The Good News is the basis for this faith. We are accepted as we are, when it appears that we shouldn't be. We can *see* that we do not meet the conditions. Yet we have faith that we are accepted. Likewise we can believe that we are going forward—shortening this or that gap between the *is* and the *should*—when it would appear that the opposite is true. Walking by sight we see only the snapshot of the present moment. The picture is tantamount to a cross-section view of a moving process. It is certainly not the equivalent of the process which carries on into an unseen future. In contrast to what we seem to assume, the present is not an accurate forecast of the future. It is just as likely to be in contrast to the future. Discontinuity even more than continuity characterizes the transition of present into future. It is simply not sensible to identify the snapshot with the total process.

The *kairos* dimension of time is not always discernible at the moment. The snapshot may not pick it up. Yet it still is present. You can believe this, though you do not *see* it. Some may call such believing without seeing an illusion. Yet it is actually what is meant by trusting in God.

In the midst of frustration, when we seem to be going only in circles, we can still commit our frustration to God. Our prayer would be something like this: "God, so far as

I can see, I'm beat. But my thoughts are not necessarily your thoughts, nor are my ways necessarily your ways. So take over! I offer my problem to you since it is too much for me."

When asking for God's help, we need still to carry out our own responsibilities. It is not honest to ask him to help if we neglect our obvious opportunities. To call upon God as an escape from our own painful efforts distorts the Good News. "When I turn things over to God," said an acquaintance of mine, "I try to make sure that I leave no stone *unturned* in using whatever possibilities are before me."

But there are those times when we do see things happen. Being reconciled to the negative, we are in a position to break its hold over us. The power inherent in the Good News makes it possible to change. We can—we will experience victories. You may be aware of this from your own experience. You may recall the time when you did not follow the ruts formed by repetition. Through some integrating power, you surprised even yourself in breaking precedent. You felt good about it—and your self-respect was enhanced.

Perhaps, however, you experience only the *hope* for victory. If so, your hope will be realized. You, too, will know victory. When these victories are experienced, they do not replace the walk by faith. Rather, they are a fulfillment of it. Such victories are exhilarating experiences. They fill us with good feelings. "The old has passed away, behold, the new has come" (II Cor. 5:17). Things have changed. Our *kairos* has come. It will come!

8. The Ideal and The Real

When you don't like yourself, you need assurance that your condition is not permanent. You need hope for the future—faith in the possibility of change. The Good News contains this hope. *Kairos* can enter into *chronos*. The gap between the *should* and the *is* in your life is not fixed. It can be bridged because God's acceptance keeps the *should* (the ideal) and the *is* (the real) together in a constructive rather than a destructive tension.

1. *Influencing your Future*

The change most needed is in the way you look at yourself. Because you are accepted in the *is*—as you are—you can look at the ideal without the usual predisposition to depression. Why? Because you are not being evaluated by the ideal. Your acceptance is not contingent upon your reaching it. You can look also at the real—the way *you* are or the way *things* are—because you are not being evaluated by it, either. There is no need to run, deny or become depressed. In the words of the Good News, "There is therefore now no condemnation for those who are in Christ Jesus" (Rom. 8:1). You can look at the real *in hope*. This means you can accept the real without losing sight of the ideal—the goal.

The tension between the real and the ideal continues, but in a constructive way. Guilt no longer fixes the gap between the *should* and the *is*. In fact, guilt becomes a stimulus to closing it. Rather than being a solution to the gap, the elimination of guilt would be a tragic loss to our humanity. Despite all the bad things said about it, guilt is an indication that we care about values, care about our self and others. Guilt's destructive tendencies, however, need to be eliminated. Through its potential for reconciliation, the Good News contains the means for converting guilt to a constructive tension.

As a constructive tension, guilt is our friend rather than our enemy. It is our built-in stimulus for change. As the indicator of the gap between the *is* and the *should*, guilt is also an impetus to closing the gap. When you feel guilty, you are aware—painfully—of your need for change.

Though guilt is potentially our friend, it still needs to be evaluated. Is it indicating where you could change things for the better? Then it needs to be taken seriously. Is it a habitual reaction whose principle purpose is to create pain? Then it needs to be taken with a grain of salt. Does your guilt pattern move you to attempt to ease the pain by making this or that concession? Such concessions may reduce the discomfort, but at the expense of your freedom. The price is too high.

As a positive tension, guilt points us toward the future rather than riveting us to the past. In moving us to change what needs to be changed, its purpose is to restore our self-respect. "Forgetting what lies behind and straining forward to what lies ahead, I press on toward the goal for the prize of the upward call of God in Christ Jesus" (Phil. 3:13–14). This is how St. Paul described his freedom. The past is a reality. We can't change it. We can only change

our attitude toward it. Yet it is this potential that constitutes our freedom. It prevents our past from determining
our future. The words *goal* and *prize* point to the future
and embody the concept of the ideal. The future, thus, is
opened to the possibilities of the perfect in contrast to the
present in which the real is something short of the ideal.

Goals can inspire us. They also can destroy us. The difference lies in the relationship of the goal to our own security. If achieving the goal is necessary for our self-
acceptance, it has the power to destroy. If, on the other
hand, our self-acceptance is secured in something other
than the goal, we are free to pursue the goal for its own
sake. An illustration of this difference is the contrast between being a perfectionist and being inspired by perfection as a goal. A perfectionist is one who cannot accept
himself, and therefore cannot like himself unless he
achieves perfection. Since the perfect is more an ideal
than a reality, the perfectionist is constantly falling short
—is always something less than acceptable to himself.

Beside keeping himself miserable, the perfectionist also
finds himself blocked in his achievements. Take as an
example a student who was consistently plagued with in-
completes in his grades. Whenever he had to write a report
or paper, he could not finish it. In fact, it was hard even
to work on it.

What was his problem? He was afraid of submitting an
inferior paper. Consequently, he was super-critical of anything he wrote, often tearing it up. To avoid being judged
by his paper, he simply frustrated his own attempts to
complete it. At least an incomplete was no judgment on
his basic ability.

What is his solution? It is to complete *something* and
submit it to his teacher. He needs to break through the

impasse in this way, even if the paper is not his best. This is the beginning of what it means to accept his limitations—to accept himself.

Painful though it is, reality needs to be accepted. We begin where we are in order to move in the direction of our goals. The goal is a challenge rather than a foreboding judgment. It is a vision of the perfect. Because we have it, we are more likely to approach it.

Forgetting what lies behind, we press on toward what lies ahead. How do we forget the past with its chronic fears of inferiority based on many painful experiences and situations? By will power? Can we will ourselves to forget? Is this not one way to keep the past alive? If what we try to remember we easily forget, then what we try to forget we may end up remembering. If we succeed, we may have repressed the matter, rather than really having forgotten it.

Forgetting occurs naturally, rather than through force. We can forget the past because we are reconciled to it. Then its memories fade because we are released from their hold.

Arthur Miller's play, *After the Fall*, has as its setting the mind of the principle character, Quentin, in which the memories of his past come and go. They seem all related to a terrible moment when his mother mercilessly castigated his father—emasculated him before his son's eyes—for losing their money in the stock market during the depression. At the climax of her tirade, she called him an idiot. For Quentin this word came to epitomize all that was evil or threatening. Later when in the grip of a hostile impulse he attempted to murder his wife, he realized the idiot was inside of him. In making his peace with his traumatic past, Quentin said, "The wish to kill is never killed, but with some gift of courage, one may look into its face when it appears, and with a stroke of love—as to an idiot in the house—forgive it again and again—forever." *

When through the Good News we become reconciled to our past and the feelings that stem from it, we can embrace it rather than being repelled by it. Its power to humiliate us is broken, as we come "with confidence" to the "throne of grace." God loves your total person—not just the good in you. If he can embrace your past and your feelings about it, so can you!

Tensions remain, of course, but they are now constructive. "Not that I have already arrived or am already perfect," says Paul, "but I press on to make it [the ideal] my own, because Christ Jesus has made me His own" (Phil. 3:12). The tension of guilt is particularly helpful in offering answers to pertinent questions. Wherein do we lack? How have we erred—sinned? What is the direction in which we should move for growth? "I press on"—not driven by guilt, but inspired by the love of God in Jesus Christ in which I am accepted, loved, as I am.

There is a world of difference between being driven by guilt and taking our cue from guilt. The former is the compulsive atoning process of the perfectionist and the latter is a means of sensitizing ourselves to the values we have chosen.

Guilt is no longer a debilitating influence because the Good News places our worth in our person, not in our performance. Performances are comparative and therefore competitive, while persons are not. Each of us is unique. Personality, however, is something else. He has an "at-

* Arthur Miller, "After the Fall." *Saturday Evening Post*, Feb. 1, 1964, page 58.

tractive personality," we say, or she has a "poor personality," or even "*no*" personality." Personality is like an achievement—it can be described by comparative qualities, perhaps even measured. Tests like the Minnesota Multiphasic Personality Inventory provide a profile which can be evaluated and compared with other profiles. Not so our person. Beyond analysis, it can only be *known*.

Actually one's personality may give little clue to his person. Skilled confidence men, for example, have attractive personalities which deceive others. We call such people "sociopathic." In spite of their deceptive appearance, they rarely have any consciousness of guilt. As we might suspect, therefore, they also have little awareness of their own persons. As Quentin says in *After the Fall*, it takes "some gift of courage" to see ourselves as we are. It is an adventure to know a person—unique and incomparable. By the same token, it is an adventure—frightening and yet thrilling—to know our self.

2. *From Microcosm to Macrocosm*

Experiencing this change in the microcosm—the world of our own person—places us in a good position to do something about the conflict between the *is* and the *should* in the macrocosm—the world of human society in which we live. As one who is "rooted and grounded in love," you have a distinct advantage in effecting change in our society. You can afford to fail! Your security rests on something other than your accomplishments. You *begin* as a person of worth—you don't have to prove it.

While the Good News helps us to take failure, it does not help us to like it. Nobody wants to fail, unless he is satisfying his low self-image. Nor do we enjoy failure.

You will be discouraged like anybody else. But you will bounce back. Your hope is centered in God and not in a particular project. The God of the Good News is the God who brings life out of death. What was more final in failure than Jesus' crucifixion? Yet it turned out to be neither final nor a failure. Your God is the God of the resurrection. Because you can afford to fail, you also can benefit from it.

Joe never knew failure. A good athlete, he was popular with the girls. When he ran for a school office, he won. He made good grades—as good as he wanted. Then he met Julie. As usual he had no trouble getting a date. But something happened that had not happened before. He fell in love with her. Julie, however, had her reservations. Joe was a fun date and a real status symbol, but was he the sort she wanted to marry?

To Joe's utter amazement, she decided he wasn't. Knowing how he felt about her, she thought it best to break off. Joe couldn't believe it. He kept calling her to ask why. Her explanation made no sense to him.

Shaken to his depths, Joe no longer was the confident, mildly cocky guy. Having never known failure, he found it more than he could take. He dropped out of school, tried drugs, and got into scrapes with the law. Through the persistent efforts of a good friend, he finally came out of it. Joe is better prepared now to cope with disappointment and to face his future realistically.

In our efforts in the macrocosm, we also can afford to be persistent. Results may not be readily forthcoming. Yet here, too, things can be happening even when it seems they are not. We are sustained by something other than our sight, namely, our faith. Progress is not always measured by the same yardstick. In fact, we may at times not be able to measure it at all. People for whom "faith is the assurance of things hoped for, the conviction of things not seen," are not given either to quitting or to planting bombs when nothing seems to change. So hang in there!

When we persist in our efforts to effect change in our society, we are predisposing ourselves to conflict. There will be opposition. This can be most unpleasant, particularly for those who have not come to grips with their problems in the microcosm. Their tendency is to project these onto the conflict in the macrocosm. When we are reconciled with ourselves, there is less need for opposition upon which to externalize our inner hostilities. We know from experience that evil does not center in the establishment or in any external symbol of the devil. Rather, we all participate in evil as human beings. When we can embrace our own evil, we can accept the evil in others. We can see the problems of society more realistically, while still holding to the vision of the ideal.

Even if you have bonafide enemies, that is, those who actively oppose you, you are in a position, because of the Good News, to actually love them. The ancient collect used frequently with the liturgical vesper service contains the petition, "Defend us from the fear of our enemies," rather than, "Defend us from our enemies." It is our fear of our enemies that gives them whatever power they have over us, and also that moves us to hate them in return. If we can be defended from the fear of our enemies, are they any longer our enemies?

Some people today are arming themselves with guns to defend themselves from their fear. Others are taking drugs. What they fear is their aloneness. Faith is the awareness that one is not alone. It is an inner relationship that joins you with the God who raised Jesus from the dead. Human enemies in this context are not so threatening. Instead of reacting in hate toward them as a defense against our fear, we can respond in ways that "heap coals of fire upon their heads." Only those who are defended from the fear of their enemies can love their enemies.

In his great chapter on love, St. Paul says, "Love never ends" (I Cor. 13:8). It never ends because it keeps open the channels of communication. Rather than polarizing, it brings together. Rather than attacking another's worth, it functions through respect.

9. A Healthy Self-Image

In the beginning of this book we concentrated on the low self-image—the picture you have of yourself when you don't like yourself. We have now reached the point where we can concentrate together on self-respect. Is self-respect the same as a positive or high self-image? If so, is such a self-image the same as conceit?

The low self-image indicates that we are unacceptable to ourselves. Conceit, on the other hand, makes us unacceptable to others. In fact, conceit is so socially unacceptable that most of us would go to great lengths to show we are not conceited. Such efforts are more likely to lead to "false modesty" than to humility.

1. A Realistic Acceptance

A conceited person is one who, in the words of Scripture, "thinks of himself more highly than he ought to think." Rather than accepting himself as he really is, he feels compelled to compensate for a low self-image. Like the low self-image, the supposedly high self-image of the conceited person is a distorted perception of the self.

The self-image that is based on self-respect is something other than conceit. One approaches himself differently when he respects himself than when he is trying to compensate for what he cannot accept. Rather than being based on standards of evaluation, self-respect is based on a given acceptance. One's worth as a person is assumed, rather than having to be proved. Conceit, on the other hand, depends upon illusions. The "positive picture" results from blocking out the negative. The low self-image also depends upon illusions. When we openly reject ourselves, we screen out the positive aspects of our person so that only a distortedly negative picture remains.

Self-respect is based on the Good News rather than upon illusions. If one is loved unconditionally by God, he can assume his worth as a person. He is not compelled to be dominant, right, competent, successful or applauded by others before he can respect himself. He can afford to be honest. Therefore, the picture he has of himself is more likely to correspond with reality.

When we view ourselves from the vantage point of respect, we see the same built-in limitations as when we view ourselves from the disadvantaged position of rejection. The difference in how we interpret what we see is a manifestation of our freedom. Obviously we also are highly influenced by our past experiences. As we are not free from such influences, so also we are not completely determined by them. Our freedom is exercised in the manner in which we approach our lack of freedom—our limitations. The fact that we are limited by various factors does not determine the attitude we take toward these limits.

Actually it is difficult to discern what our limitations are. So many influences may be involved in any particular situation that we never can know for certain that we have reached the end of our potential. In fact, the evidence indicates that we rarely even approach our potential, let alone fulfill it. The fact remains, however, that we may encounter more handicaps than assets in achieving a goal.

The Christian tradition takes full cognizance of these limitations. In the area of values and their fulfillment, the hindering influence is called the *flesh*. Flesh normally refers to the physical body. In this use of the term, however, it refers to the negative quality of the human spirit. We see its effect in the hatreds, jealousies, exploitations, brutalities and betrayals that plague human society. As a factor at work within us, the flesh produces ambivalence; that is, it constitutes an opposing will.

When there are two opposing forces in the same person, the effect is disintegrating. To the extent that this disintegration takes place, his efforts naturally are hindered. He lacks that total effort that one will can provide. The desire to achieve is frustrated.

Human error, human carelessness, and human sin all are related in varying degrees to this debilitating ambivalence. Its cumulative effect can be overwhelming, leaving us with only the futility of our own impotence. "I do not understand my own actions. For I do not do what I want, but I do the very thing I hate" (Rom. 7:15). I imagine you can understand this lament of St. Paul. Most of us know what it is like to be painfully preoccupied with our inadequacy. "I can't do anything right!"

When we agonize in this way over our inadequacy, we are showing how little we accept inadequacy as our destiny. The conflict we have over it is an evidence of our freedom. We protest our limitations. Protest is one expression of freedom. Positive action is another. Limitations in themselves do not negate our freedom. Choice still remains! How shall I respond to my limitations? Here is where the Good News of the grace of God enters the picture.

As unconditional love, grace breaks through all limitations that would impose themselves upon the human spirit. It removes all conditions that would restrict human worth. Grace, thus, is the guarantor of human freedom, providing the confidence we need to choose between attitudes. The same St. Paul who lamented his inability to do what he wished was able also to affirm his ability. "I can do all things in him who strengthens me" (Phil. 4:15). We are free to make such affirmations because grace has emancipated us from the low self-image with its restrictive influence. No longer is it the regulator of what we can receive. Grace has obliterated its basis for being. By establishing our acceptance as unconditional, grace provides us with the basis for the development, instead, of self-respect.

In contrast to the restricting influence of the low self-image, the positive self-image that constitutes self-respect has an openness to receive that is potentially unlimited. It is precisely this openness that characterizes the attitude of faith. Though faith's openness is potentially unlimited, it is still a realistic approach. Because it is faith, it includes the possibility of failure. Otherwise it would be an illusion.

2. The Mutuality of Respect

The title of this chapter contains a frequent coupling of words. Actually the adjective, "healthy," is unnecessary, since self-respect is healthy in itself. Evidently the word, "healthy," is used to make it clear that self-respect is not self-conceit.

When you respect yourself, you encourage others to respect you, also. Your attitude toward yourself is contagious. Perhaps you have heard it said of one who is being mistreated, "Well, he asks for it!" In other words, he seems to have a need for abuse and puts himself in the position to receive such treatment. Had he respect for himself, he would behave differently toward others.

When you respect yourself, you have the resources for respecting others. Again it is your attitude toward yourself that is contagious: it affects your attitude toward others. The biblical admonition, "You shall love your neighbor as yourself," could be paraphrased, "You shall respect your neighbor as yourself." This mutuality between attitudes toward self and neighbor is expressed by the psychiatrist, Thomas Harris, as, "I'm okay, you're okay." * The way my neighbor treats me affects my attitude toward myself. On the other hand, my attitude toward myself affects the way I treat my neighbor—and also the way my neighbor treats me.

3. The People of God

This mutuality in the giving and receiving of respect makes it obvious that self-respect is not achieved in isolation. Although the Good News is about God's approach to us, self-respect is not realized through our relationship with God alone. Nor is it achieved through private study of the Bible, as important as this is. Self-respect is not achieved without involvement in human interaction.

From the beginning of recorded history, religion has been a group affair. The Christian Way is no exception. The Old and New Testaments concern the people of God. In the Old Testament these people are called Israel; in the New Testament, the church.

* Thomas Harris, I'm Okay, You're Okay. New York: Harper and Row, 1967.

There was a "loner" movement in the early years of the Christian era, but it did not survive. To escape the wickedness of the world some devout individuals took to solitary places like the desert to live alone. The best remembered of these persons is Simon Stylites, who obtained his name by the unusual way in which he separated himself from the world. He positioned himself on top of a pole 60 feet high where he lived for 30 years. Of course, he was not really alone because his followers had to supply him with food by ladder. In fact, Simon preached from his pillar to people who came to hear him, and actually was very influential in the Christian community.

The loner, however, began to disappear and, instead, people of like desires gathered together to form their own groups. They established monasteries and nunneries. The monastic movement proved far more popular than going it alone. In their own communities, the monks and nuns provided each other with the human relationships we all seem to need to develop our sense of identity.

The word, "church," means literally a group of people who are *called out*. Used generally to mean a public assembly, the word was used by Christians to designate their own group as it gathered together for worship and fellowship. The Good News draws people together to share in the love of God. The Apostle's Creed calls the church the "communion of saints." A saint is one who is set apart for God. He is called out by the Good News to love his neighbor as Christ has loved him. Being set apart to love, he is moved to join with others who become the objects of his love. Mutuality exists here also. We receive the love of God through the love of God's people. At the same time, receiving the love of God motivates us to love others.

There are endless witnesses to the power of love. I would

like to share just one of these—one of recent and personal impact. The father of a student of mine was robbed and murdered by three young men whom he picked up as hitchhikers. His wife—the mother of my student—wrote an "open letter to the three boys who murdered my husband." It was published in the newspaper shortly after the funeral. She wrote:

> "During the past three days my grief and desolation have been eased and comforted by the love and faith of so many wonderful friends and relatives. But, in the midst of all this, and especially in the quiet moments, my thoughts keep turning to you three. You may feel that you are men, but to me you are just boys—like my own sons—and I wonder to whom you are turning for comfort and strength and reassurance.
>
> "I suppose I will never know what motivated your actions that night, but if the shots were fired out of sheer panic, my heart aches for you and I wish there were only some way I could help you in what you must be suffering now. If hate made you pull that trigger, I can only pray that you can come to know the love of God that fills the heart and leaves no room for hate. If you were under the influence of drugs, please, for my sake and your own, don't waste your lives, too. Get help and rid yourselves of that stuff.
>
> "Please, if you see this, find a church someplace where you can be alone; then read this again. Know that God forgives you and that my family and I forgive you—then go out and make something worthwhile of the rest of your lives.
>
> "God keep and bless you."

This is the kind of difference in human living that the Good News makes possible.

4. The Lord's Supper

The Lord's Supper is the symbolic expression of the intimacy of the Christian fellowship. The setting is like a family meal in which the gathered group is the family of the Lord. We begin our life in the family setting and continue it in families or family-like groups. In the service, the people of God gather around the table of the Lord to share together in bread and wine (or grape juice). The importance of this ritual is that they actually are sharing together in the symbols of reconciliation—the body and blood of Christ. Through the elements of physical sustenance, the dynamic process of reconciliation is symbolized in relationship to God—it is his atonement. It is symbolized in relationship to ourselves—the elements are ingested. It is symbolized in relationship to other people—we share the same cup, or the same elements of the communion service. The service's important place in Christian worship indicates the recurring human need for reconciliation and reassurance.

The human response to the Good News has given to the Lord's Supper one of its earliest names, the "eucharist," which means "thanksgiving." This name points to the positive attitude toward life and our involvement in it that the Good News generates. It is to this involvement that we give our attention in the concluding chapter.

10. Your Involvement

We have come to the last chapter. What yet remains to be said? If we were playing a game, I would say, "It's your move." What remains is your involvement. This book, hopefully, stimulated some ideas for you. Perhaps you were affected in other ways as well. If we have struck up something between us, we have approximated a counseling relationship.

No matter how involved one becomes in reading a book, the relationship with the author is always something less than a personal relationship. Perhaps you are meeting now with a counselor. He may have referred this book to you. If so, I hope it has been helpful to your counseling relationship. If you are not seeing a counselor, you might consider doing so, particularly if you are aware of obstacles that may prevent you from taking hold. From the viewpoint of this book, your pastor is the most likely person to be your counselor.

Even counseling, however, still falls short of what I mean by your involvement. Like the reading of this book, the counseling relationship helps you become involved. This is why we now have come to your move.

1. Participator rather than Spectator

In many ways ours is a spectator age. Rather than participating ourselves, we identify vicariously with those who do. Consider the millions of people who regularly watch professional and college sports on television. Consider the millions more who go to the movies and become involved with the action on the screen—all the while sitting in their seats. We may even remain spectators in church. In her newspaper advice column, Dear Abby, in making a suggestion regarding crying babies in church, referred to the congregation as "the audience." The person in the pew, thus, is considered the passive observer or recipient of what is going on up front. No doubt this is the case with many people. Yet it is not what the church is about. We are *called out* not as spectators but as participators.

The Lord's Supper is a symbolic example of this participation. You cannot very well be a part of a fellowship meal without taking some action. While churches have different ways of celebrating communion each person has a function. He is involved. In doing so he is demonstrating his role as a functioning member of the "Body of Christ," St. Paul's name for the church.

2. *The Mutuality Process of Give-and-Take*

You are not going to like yourself any better by being a spectator. Too many of your basic needs will remain unsatisfied. These needs are met as you tap your potential by involving yourself in the process of giving and receiving. Giving is obviously an action. Yet so is receiving. In fact, for some it is a very difficult action. Because they are more obnoxious, we usually hear more about persons who find it difficult to give. We resent their one-sidedness and call them sponges.

In contrast, those who find it difficult to receive often are praised for being unselfish. If it is more blessed to give than to receive, as the Scripture says, those who insist on being givers only are hogging all the blessings. Obviously, if giving is an obligation, so also is receiving. Those who insist on being givers only, disrupt the mutuality process as much as those who insist on being receivers only. Each is depriving the other.

We find it easier to understand why someone would be reluctant to give. Either he has not been encouraged to make his contribution or he is too insecure to do so. But why would anyone resist receiving? Aren't we only too glad to be on the receiving end? Not necessarily. Some of us feel uncomfortable when we receive. Unless we can quickly restore the balance by giving in return, we feel guilty. Others have a fear of obligation. If they receive something, they feel indebted. Because such obligations have been painful experiences in the past, they avoid what seems to be an attempt to put them in this position again. To some of us the one who gives is in the superior position. This puts the receiver in the inferior position. By persisting in being only the giver, one holds on to the superior position.

What is needed to break through these resistances is grace. Our low self-image limits both our giving and receiving. Grace does away with these limits. It puts aside all questions of deserving. Your worth is not based on your goodness or rightness. Nor is it denied by your badness or wrongness. You are loved by God not for your goodness but for yourself. You are accepted as you are and not on conditions imposed by your self-image. Grace offers this acceptance. Your reception of it is needed to complete the contract—or covenant, as it traditionally is called. The result is your emancipation from all limitations on receiving. Yet this is only part of your involvement.

When the limits imposed by our self-image are removed,

we are free to give. The purpose for which you are *called
out* can now be affirmed. As the recipient of God's grace,
you are equipped—set apart—for doing. Your needs are
not satisfied simply by receiving. You need also to give.
Receiving prepares you for giving.

We establish our identity by contributing of ourselves.
Until we contribute, our identity is unaffirmed. Human
needs are fulfilled through interdependence, not by dependence or independence. We need others. We need, also,
to be needed by others. This is the mutuality process. It
is now your move to get involved in this process.

You may feel guilty about fulfilling your own needs
when you give of yourselves to this or that cause or service.
You may be as interested in the fact that it is *you* who are
doing the service as in the service itself. As you accept this
reality, you will realize that mixed motivation, even in
altruistic enterprises, is inevitable. You will do a better
job in directing your efforts if you accept your mixed
motives than if you feel called upon to deny them in order
to fortify your confidence.

3. *Liberated from Paralysis*

Once you are liberated from the paralysis of will caused
by the low self-image, you are ready for involvement.
There is a risk, however. In being involved you also can
be hurt, disappointed, rejected. You may fail as well as
achieve. This is why some people prefer to remain de-
tached. They are protecting themselves from hurt and
failure. Although they are wrong in their course of action,
they are right in their deduction. There is no "no-risk"
insurance for our involvements. The outcome is uncertain.
Success is not guaranteed. The outcome is certain, however,

for those who remain aloof. They will fulfill less and less of their potential. Their enjoyment of life will decrease as their passions dissipate in the paucity of their vision. Having traded all for safety, they will be left only with their apathy.

4. Expression of Caring

Becoming involved is an expression of caring. A human being created in God's image is a being who cares. He is concerned about himself, about God, about his neighbor, and about the world. Our society is in danger of losing all semblance of community because people are frightened and withdraw into their own little fortresses of safety. In our day of violence there is reason to be frightened. Yet in attempting to save their lives, they may lose their humanity. By drawing their curtains, literally and figuratively, on what is happening to their neighbor, they sabotage their own development as persons.

In contrast, those who care and show it are fulfilling their own needs as well. It is a marvelous experience to know that someone cares about you. In contrast, it is a miserable experience to wonder whether anybody cares at all. By the same token, it is a marvelous experience to show another person that you care. If he can receive it, his sense of worth is increased. He feels valued. You, in turn, experience the blessedness of giving. In expressing your care, you fulfill your own humanity. You satisfy your own need for worth and affirm your identity.

So take it from there. It's your turn to move in some direction—to become involved in some group—to be active in some concern. Your church is the logical place to begin. If not there, look elsewhere. The beginnings may be small, the involvement less than you desire. Stay with it and see where it takes you.

There is Good News. Affirm it for yourself. Believe in God. Believe in yourself. Believe in your neighbor. Hope!